ZONDERKIDZ

One Lost Sheep
Copyright © 2007 by Rhonda Gowler Greene
Illustrations © 2014 by Margaret Spengler

This title is also available as a Zondervan ebook.
Visit www.zondervan.com/ebooks.

Requests for information should be addressed to:

Zonderkidz, 5300 *Patterson Ave SE, Grand Rapids, Michigan* 49530

ISBN 978-0-310-73178-8

Editor: Barbara Herndon
Art direction & design: Mary pat Pino

Printed in China

14 15 16 17 18 /LPC/ 10 9 8 7 6 5 4 3 2 1

One Lost Sheep

Rhonda Gowler Greene
Illustrated by Margaret Spengler

ZONDER**kidz**

With love, for Gary, whom I can always count on.
—RGG

For my two favorite guys: Ken, my loving husband
and Matt, my amazing son.

—MS

Then Jesus told them this parable:
"*Suppose one of you has a hundred sheep and loses
one of them. Doesn't he leave the ninety-nine in the
open country and go after the lost sheep until he finds it?*"
Taken from **Luke 15:3–4**

White and wooly,
hungry sheep
grazing by a mountain, steep.

Shepherd watching
them with care,
guards each one from beast and bear.

Counts to make sure all are there ...

One, two,
three, four,
five, six, even more ...

Big ones, small ones,
ewes and rams,
brothers, sisters, little lambs ...

... ninety-eight,
ninety-nine,
one hundred sheep.
Yes, all are fine.

Shepherd leads
his flock of sheep
to clear, cool stream
past mountain, steep.

Down the path
clip-clop they go,
stepping sure, stepping slow.

Uh-oh!
One begins to stray.
Little lamb,
don't lose your way!

Clip ... clop
up mountain, steep.
Baa ... baa ... one lost sheep.

Now shepherd counts
just ninety-nine.
One lost sheep,
he must find!

Step,
   step,
      step
up mountain, steep.
Where, oh where, is that lost sheep?

By the tree?
No, not there.
Searching,
searching everywhere ...

In the brambles?
No, not there.
Searching,
searching everywhere ...

Behind those rocks?
No, not there.
Searching,
searching everywhere ...

Listen ... Shhh ...
That wayward lamb
bleating *Baa baa*, here I am.

Shepherd lifts
that sheep up high,
rejoices with a happy sigh.

Carries it
down mountain, steep,
safe and sound
now in his keep.

Shares his gladness
all around,
tells his friends
his sheep is found.

White and wooly,
sleepy sheep
dozing by a mountain, steep.

Shepherd watching
through the night
as the stars shine
brilliant-bright.

Like that shepherd, God above
keeps us in his boundless love.

The Lord God is our shepherd too,
watching over ...
me and you.